# The Lending (

CW00427831

## How the world s largest peer to peer lender is transforming finance and how you can benefit

by Peter Renton
Founder
Lend Academy

To gain more understanding of peer to peer lending please subscribe to our newsletter here:
http://www.lendacademy.com/subscribe

Thanks for purchasing this book. Please tell the world what you think by reviewing it on Amazon. By providing feedback I can make the next version even better. And thanks again.

# Table of Contents

**Preface**................................................................**5**

Disclaimer ...............................................................6

**Foreword** ...........................................................**8**

Lending Club Fever ..................................................8

No Battle Plan Survives Contact With The Enemy .......9

**Chapter 1 – Introduction** ...............................**10**

What is Lending Club? .............................................10

*P2P Lending* ..........................................................*10*

*The World's Largest P2P Lender*..............................*11*

How the Platform Works..........................................12

*For Investors*.........................................................*12*

*For Borrowers*.......................................................*12*

Why P2P Lending is Becoming Popular......................13

*Advantages for Investors*.......................................*14*

*Advantages for Borrowers*......................................*15*

**Chapter 2 – History of Lending Club**............**17**

The Germination of an Idea.....................................17

The Opportunity......................................................18

Raising Capital........................................................19

Launching on Facebook ...........................................21

Beyond Facebook....................................................22

SEC Registration and The Quiet Period......................22

The Financial Crisis.................................................24

Consolidating Their Position ....................................25

The Birth of LC Advisors and the Attraction of Large Investors ...........26

In 2012 the Floodgates Opened................................26

**Chapter 3 – Lending Club Investors**.............**28**

Investor Eligibility..................................................28

Lending Club Prospectus..........................................30

Types of Investor Accounts ......................................30

*Standard Investment Accounts*................................*30*

*Retirement Accounts* .............................................*30*

*Lending Club PRIME Accounts*................................*31*

*Other Account Types*..............................................*31*

Investor Fees..........................................................31

The Investment Platform..........................................33

*Automated Loan Picking With the Portfolio Builder*.................................*33*
*Selecting Loans Manually*.................................*34*
*Loan Filtering*.................................*35*
*Net Annualized Return*.................................*36*
*Portfolios and Account Details*.................................*37*
Third Party Investor Tools .................................38
Diversification.................................39
Investment Returns .................................40
The Trading Platform.................................41
LC Advisors.................................42
Collection Practices for Late Loans.................................43
Tax Liability on Lending Club Investments.................................45
Investor Profiles.................................45
*Phillip McFarland*.................................*46*
*Larry Ludwig*.................................*47*
*Megan Nitz*.................................*49*

**Chapter 4 – Lending Club Borrowers**.................................**51**
Eligibility .................................51
Loan Purposes.................................52
An Explanation of Lending Club Loan Grades and Interest Rates.................................53
Considerations Before Applying for a Lending Club Loan.................................54
Borrower Loan Fees .................................56
*Origination Fee*.................................*56*
*Late Payment Fee*.................................*57*
*Unsuccessful Payment Fee*.................................*57*
*Check Processing Fee*.................................*57*
How the Borrowing Process Works at Lending Club.................................58
The Loan Funding Process.................................61
Borrower Profiles .................................63
*Alex Taguchi*.................................*63*
*Dan Bradford*.................................*64*
*Zachary Knight*.................................*65*

**Chapter 5 – The Future**.................................**67**
The Near Term Challenges .................................67
*Becoming a Mainstream Investment*.................................*67*
*The States Problem*.................................*68*
*Institutional Versus Retail Investors*.................................*69*
*Getting to Profitability*.................................*69*
Long Term Opportunities.................................70
*Future Product Lines* .................................*70*

*The Lending Club IPO*.........................................................................71
*A Trillion Dollar Company*..............................................................72

**About The Author** ....................................................**73**

# Preface

I have always loved investing. But I have never been much of a risk-taker; I preferred the buy and hold strategy rather than active trading. My favorite investments were those that kept going up steadily month after month. The trouble was after the financial crisis of 2008-09 those kinds of investments were hard to find.

I first read an article about peer-to-peer lending in 2008 after I had sold my second business. It seemed like an intriguing idea but I didn't think any more about it. Then in the winter of 2009 when it seemed like the financial world was falling apart I remembered that article, so I did a little research. And I discovered Lending Club.

At the time I was looking for something that had the potential of a good investment return but without the crazy volatility that we had been seeing in the stock and bond markets. The more I read about Lending Club the more I liked the idea, so after some deliberation I opened an account. That was June 2009.

Like many investors I started off with a very small amount – just $500. Then after Lending Club had earned my trust I added $10,000. I knew no other Lending Club investors whatsoever but the idea of investing directly in borrowers appealed to me. In 2010 I decided that I needed to get more serious about Lending Club so I opened an IRA in my name and my wife's name and added substantially to my investment. By late 2012 I had over $100,000 invested in Lending Club across four different accounts.

In the fall of 2010 I found myself looking for a new business opportunity. I had sold my last business in 2008 and my contract with the new buyers was over by the middle of 2010. After taking the summer off to just relax with my family I was looking for something new and different.

That was when I noticed a blog for sale called
SocialLending.net. It was all about this new industry of peer to
peer lending, one that I had grown to believe in over the
previous 18 months. So, I bought the blog and started writing
about this burgeoning new industry.

The blog is now called LendAcademy.com and I have written
hundreds of articles about Lending Club and the industry in
general. The more I learn about peer to peer lending the more
excited I am for its future. I truly believe that Lending Club is
going to change the world and I am excited to be playing a
small part in it. By reading this book you will gain a greater
understanding about this remarkable company and why it is
destined to rewrite the financial landscape of this country.

If you have any questions or comments about this book please
let me know. I can be reached at peter@lendacademy.com. I
read every email I receive.

Thanks,

Peter Renton
Founder
Lend Academy
http://www.lendacademy.com/

## Disclaimer

This book is intended to provide an introduction to Lending
Club. It is for information purposes only and nothing
contained within should be considered investment advice. The
author of this book is not qualified to provide such advice –
you should always seek a qualified professional before making
any investment decisions.

The author has made every effort to provide current
information but due to the fast changing nature of the peer to

peer lending industry no guarantee can be made as to the accuracy of the information contained within.

# Foreword

## Lending Club Fever

I met Peter two years ago, not long after he first learned about Lending Club and began investing.  His initial intrigue quickly became a passion, and he has become one of the most respected experts in Lending Club matters. His blog Lendacademy.com is a trusted source of information, his courses educate new investors, he is frequently interviewed and quoted by major media outlets, and his new book, The Lending Club Story, is the very first book dedicated to our company. For someone who has focused his career on our business, it is amazing to note that two years ago Peter had never written a blog post about Lending Club -- much less an entire book.

Other Lending Club investors have become employees, Board members, equity investors, Lending Club fund managers and advisors. Many have become friends. All have become our best marketers and evangelists. At Lending Club we came up with a name to describe the state of mind that new investors find themselves into when they come to realize the extraordinary efficiency and transformative power of the Lending Club model and decide to quit their day job, write a blog, send us their resume and call us to share new product ideas: we call it Lending Club fever.

I was lucky enough to be the first reported case of Lending Club fever in the summer of 2006 and haven't found (or looked for) a cure since. That summer I realized how the financial system had become focused on itself rather than its customers, and how consumer lending could be made so much more efficient and deliver so much more value.

# No Battle Plan Survives Contact With The Enemy

While Lending Club today remains true to the original idea of creating a platform that efficiently connects investors and borrowers, the implementation has differed widely from the initial sketch and has evolved rapidly. Through a process of adaptation, data gathering, market feedback, learning and evolution Lending Club is quickly becoming more relevant to more people.

We launched in 2007 as a Facebook application based on the idea that the social graph would help establish trusted connections among members. As we reached $1 billion in personal loans on November 5th, 2012, less than $2 million had been sourced through our Facebook application. We will continue to innovate and break new grounds, launch new products and invent new services, and will probably do so in ways we cannot even foresee today. I am grateful that we have the constant feedback from the market to guide us, channeled by leaders like Peter.

I very much enjoyed reading Peter Renton's book, the first of its kind entirely dedicated to Lending Club. Half storytelling and half user manual, it is as captivating as it is practical. I am confident you will enjoy it as much as I did.

Renaud Laplanche
CEO and Founder
Lending Club

# Chapter 1 – Introduction

# ⠿ LendingClub

## What is Lending Club?

It goes by many names. Peer to peer lending, social lending, person-to-person lending or p2p lending are all names used to describe the industry that Lending Club operates in. But Lending Club simply calls it consumer lending which is a broad way of describing it.

Lending Club is changing the face of lending by removing the bank from the process. It operates online bringing together investors and borrowers directly so that both can benefit. The borrower benefits by getting a lower interest rate and easy access to funds and the investor benefits by earning a higher return than traditional fixed income investments.

There are no Lending Club branches, although they do have offices in downtown San Francisco. Everything is conducted online or over the phone. Because of this they have little of the huge infrastructure costs that burdens modern banking. So they can pass the savings on to the investors and borrowers.

### P2P Lending

In this book we will be using the term peer-to-peer lending (shortened to p2p lending) to describe this industry. Even though Lending Club no longer uses this term, it is still the preferred term for most investors and borrowers.

What is p2p lending exactly? It has traditionally been about a financial exchange between individuals. People who want to borrow money (borrowers) connect with people who have money to lend (investors). This is something that has happened since the invention of money thousands of years ago.

The main difference with p2p lending today is that both parties can have no relationship with each other and still have a safe and successful transaction. In the 21st century p2p lending has been brought online with websites like LendingClub.com facilitating this process between complete strangers.

## The World's Largest P2P Lender

Since its founding in 2007, Lending Club has grown to become the world's largest p2p lender crossing over $1 billion in loans issued in November 2012. In the United States Prosper.com is the main competitor to Lending Club but today Lending Club has close to an 80% market share.

Below is a chart that shows their growth from the very beginning through crossing over $1 billion in total loans issued. This chart shows total loan volume through the end of November 2012.

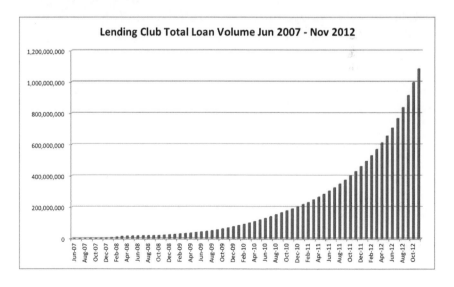

# How the Platform Works

There are two distinct parties on Lending Club and while both are absolutely necessary for the success of the platform they operate very differently.

## For Investors

Investors need to register on LendingClub.com before they can invest in borrower loans. Once an investor is registered and has funded their account they can invest in the available loans on the platform. The investor is given detailed credit information about each loan as well as limited personal information (such as income and place of residence) about the borrower. No names, contact information or sensitive personal information is available to investors. Investors can also ask a limited set of questions to the borrower while the loan is being funded.

Investors can build a portfolio of loans (called notes) by individually selecting each loan or by using one of the tools that Lending Club provides to help automate the process. Investors typically build a portfolio based on their desired interest rate and appetite for risk – with higher interest loans typically being more risky. There are seven loan grades: A through G with A-grade loans having the lowest interest rates and G-grade loans the highest rates. Once a loan is issued the investors who funded the loan will begin receiving monthly payments within 30-45 days.

For a more detailed description of the investing process please read Chapter 3.

## For Borrowers

Borrowers apply for a loan through LendingClub.com and go through a screening process. If they pass the screening process and agree to the terms then the loan is made available to investors on the online platform. Loan terms are typically three or five years, interest rates vary from 6% to over 24% and the maximum loan amount is $35,000.

Borrowers will pay an origination fee that is between 1.11% and 5% of the loan amount. This amount comes off the total amount borrowed, so if a borrower requests $10,000 and pays a 5% origination fee then the borrower will receive $9,500 if their loan is funded at 100%. This origination fee varies based upon the loan grade that Lending Club assigns the borrower.

A loan is given two weeks on the platform to be funded by investors. If it is 100% funded before the two-week period it is removed from the platform and will start the origination process assuming it has been approved. Around 99% of loans are fully funded by investors.

For a more detailed description of the borrowing process please read Chapter 4.

## Why P2P Lending is Becoming Popular

Peer to peer lending is a rapidly growing industry. In the 12 months ending November 30, 2012 the total amount of loans issued by Lending Club was around $655 million. That is more than 150% growth over the preceding 12 months. On the next page is a chart showing the growth in monthly loan volume at Lending Club for the 18 months through November 2012. The black line is the three-month moving average. Clearly, it is becoming more popular all the time.

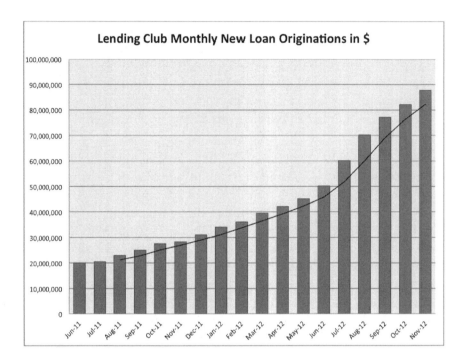

To understand why peer to peer lending is growing so fast, we need to look at the advantages it provides for both investors and borrowers.

## Advantages for Investors

There are several advantages for investors. The biggest and most important one is the high rate of return on their investment. Many Lending Club investors are averaging at least a 10% annualized return, and the vast majority are earning more than 6%.

You can choose your level of risk with p2p lending. You can choose to invest in A-grade loans where every borrower has excellent credit, so the likelihood of default is low. Or you can invest in higher risk, higher interest loans. Alternatively, you could choose some combination of these high risk and low risk loans.

Peer to peer lending also adds diversification to an investor's overall portfolio. You are investing in consumer credit, which is a different asset class from other investments. Then there is the issue of volatility or lack thereof. A well-diversified investment portfolio at Lending Club will likely grow in value every month, month after month, year after year, with none of the wild gyrations of stock market investing.

Also, many people are drawn to peer to peer lending because it is about investing in real people, not some faceless bank or mutual fund. While investors never know exactly who is behind the loans they invest in, there can be a sense of satisfaction in knowing their money is helping people.

## Advantages for Borrowers

The biggest advantage for borrowers is a lower cost of credit. Despite mortgage interest rates at record lows, credit card rates have continued to rise. This is happening despite the fact that credit card defaults have been coming down the past couple of years.

For people carrying a credit card balance they found their rates often increasing despite a good payment history. At Lending Club, in most cases interest rates are several percentage points lower than at the credit card companies.

Another advantage for borrowers is access to credit. The financial crisis had a huge impact on banks and financial institutions that is still being felt. Many individuals who had found it easy to get loans from banks before suddenly found themselves cut off.

Many people had used the equity in their home to borrow money in the past couple of decades, but with homes across the country dropping in value, banks became much more cautious with this kind of lending. At the same time unsecured personal loans from banks became almost non-existent.

Clearly, there has been a void in consumer financing and Lending Club helped fill that void. The application process is simple, it can all be done online and borrowers can find out their interest rate with just a few clicks.

The fixed loan term, three or five years, is also appealing because borrowers can see their debt will be completely paid off in a relatively short time period. For people serious about getting out of credit card debt Lending Club has provided a compelling solution.

# Chapter 2 – History of Lending Club

While Lending Club officially began operations in 2007 its roots go much further back – back to when Renaud Laplanche, the founder and CEO of Lending Club, was starting his previous company.

## The Germination of an Idea

This was back in 2000 when Laplanche was starting MatchPoint (which would later be acquired by Oracle). Like many bootstrapping entrepreneurs he used a credit card to help fund the early days of his company. It was the only time in his life that Laplanche carried a balance on his credit card.

It was the first time he realized just how expensive credit cards really were. Despite decent credit he was paying an 18% interest rate on these credit cards. It just so happened that he also borrowed money during that time from some friends and the terms he received from these friends were much more favorable than from the credit card companies. He wondered whether this idea could be developed into a model to provide a more efficient form of financing. He did nothing about it at the time, he just filed that idea away as something to consider at a later date.

After the sale of MatchPoint to Oracle in 2005 Laplanche continued to work for Oracle for a year and then in July 2006 he decided to take a one-year sabbatical. Two weeks into his sabbatical he received his credit card statement and he remembered his experience from six years earlier. Now, though, he had the time to really look into the idea.

This was now six years later, he had a longer credit history and he had recently sold a company for tens of millions of dollars. Despite that he was astonished to see that if he had decided to carry a balance on his credit card he would be paying an interest rate of 18.99%.

# The Opportunity

It became clear to Laplanche that credit card issuers do not do a lot of risk based pricing. They apply this one-size fits all interest rate across the board to their customers and simply use the good quality borrowers to subsidize the lower quality ones. So, if he could isolate the top 10% or 20% of their customer base he could offer these people a lower interest rate. Then if he could have people like his friends invest in these borrowers they could enjoy the same kind of returns as the credit card companies.

So Laplanche started doing some research. He was lucky enough to know Pete Hart, the former CEO of MasterCard, who obviously knew the credit card industry intimately and through him Laplanche was able to make contact with many former executives at MasterCard.

When Laplanche started doing his own research in July 2006 he quickly discovered that Prosper.com had already launched earlier that year with a similar model that he had envisioned. This was both bad news and good news for him. Bad news in the sense that someone had beaten him to the idea but good news in that a company was demonstrating that it could already be done. He also discovered that Zopa had launched the previous year in the UK.

Two early decisions Laplanche made were instrumental in differentiating his company from Prosper. The first was the underwriting model. At the time Prosper had a minimum credit score requirement of 520, Laplanche wanted to focus on more creditworthy borrowers. The second was the fixed price model. Prosper had an auction model where investors would decide on the interest rates they were willing to receive. Laplanche felt that letting the market decide was not the best way to set interest rates, feeling that investors did not have enough knowledge of consumer borrowing to make accurate decisions.

Laplanche needed a name for his new company. He was brainstorming with his wife one day in August 2006 when she came up with the name Lending Club. Here is his thinking behind the name:

*"While the trend currently is in favor of more evocative names, we felt very strongly that the idea was so innovative and disruptive that we should use a descriptive name that explains what it is, and brings it closer to a known concept (like a "club" where the members all benefit from the pooling of resources). We came up with about 20 names along the same lines, selected Lending Club as the winner and then started hunting down the owner [of the domain]. I started the negotiations in September 2006 and closed the acquisition of the domain name in November 2006. The acquisition price was $17,000."*

## Raising Capital

In order to kick-start the company Laplanche raised $2 million in angel financing from himself and a handful of private investors who had invested in his previous company. This fundraising occurred from October 2006 through March 2007, and was used to recruit the first 12-15 team members, obtain the necessary state licenses and build the first version of the loan origination and investment platform.

Laplanche realized, though, that to really launch the platform he would need a lot more than $2 million. He would need some strong equity partners who would be willing to invest substantially in Lending Club.

Dan Ciporin, a partner at venture capital firm Canaan Partners, was instrumental in helping to get Lending Club off the ground with venture capital financing. Ciporin first met

Laplanche through a mutual friend at a time when the idea for Lending Club was nothing more than a PowerPoint presentation.

Ciporin met Laplanche at this friend's house and watched the PowerPoint. He immediately liked Laplanche and his idea. Ciporin gave Laplanche a laundry list of things that needed to happen before his company could consider funding Lending Club. He then told Laplanche to get back in touch in six months when those tasks had been completed. Laplanche called him back in three months.

Ciporin was impressed. Laplanche had not only done everything on the list but he did it in half the time. It was then that Ciporin knew that this was a person he wanted to fund. Ciporin had worked at MasterCard and was also CEO at Shopping.com so this kind of deal was in his sweet spot. He could see the potential of Lending Club, that it could truly change the face of consumer finance.

He took it to the partners at his firm, Canaan Partners, and the biggest risk they could see was the regulatory risk. But they knew that Prosper had been operating for over a year and so the thinking was that this risk was minimal.

In the end Laplanche had a choice of several venture capital firms and he chose Canaan Partners because of Dan Ciporin and the help that he had provided to Lending Club along the way. Ciporin also joined the Lending Club board at this time.

Laplanche chose Norwest Partners as the other funding partner primarily because of their relationship with Wells Fargo that he thought could be very useful going forward. He had also come to know and like Jeff Crowe, a partner at Norwest, and thought Crowe would be a valuable addition to the Lending Club board. Together Norwest and Canaan contributed $10 million in the first Series A round.

# Launching on Facebook

Lending Club launched on Facebook on May 24, 2007 with little fanfare. Back in those days Prosper and Zopa were the leading players and few people saw the significance of the launch of another p2p lending platform.

The choice of launching as a Facebook application was an interesting one. Here is a quote from Laplanche in the original press release:

*"Person-to-person lending will gain broad adoption faster in an environment where people feel connected to each other," said Laplanche. "Facebook is the perfect launch platform, with 24 million active users who communicate and share information through the social graph, or the network of connections and relationships between people."*

At the time Laplanche believed that utilizing connections between people would enhance the adoption of p2p lending. The basic idea that p2p lending needed more trust and so would grow faster in an environment where there are existing connections and the ability to track connections.

The Facebook launch was a success from a public relations standpoint. It did help Lending Club gain some attention, as Facebook believed that Lending Club could become one of their flagship applications and a possible way for them to monetize their network. But in terms of traffic and loan volume it was not a huge success.

Part of what didn't work out is that Facebook was very much a college student network at that time. So, on the borrower side there were not many people who could meet their credit policy because they were young and had limited credit history. And on the flipside most investors didn't have a large amount of money to invest.

# Beyond Facebook

The plan was always to allow the general public to invest and borrow at Lending Club and on September 14, 2007 that became a reality. That was the date that Lending Club became available for everyone, not just Facebook users.

This was an exciting time at Lending Club. The previous month they had closed their first round of venture capital funding and p2p lending was getting great press coverage. By casting a wider net beyond Facebook users Lending Club could really start to get some traction.

Once Lending Club allowed everyone on their platform they did begin to grow very quickly. In September 2007, the first month Lending Club was widely available they issued $373,000 in new loans. Six months later, in March 2009, loan volume had grown more than 1000% to $4.2 million. Lending Club was on a roll.

# SEC Registration and The Quiet Period

When Lending Club launched, their interpretation of the financial laws was that they were functioning in a similar way to a banking intermediary. They really were just a facilitator of loans between borrowers and lenders. This was the same way that Prosper had been operating and so it was thought to be the correct interpretation of the laws.

Soon after launch, in the summer of 2007, Laplanche began a dialogue with the Securities and Exchange Commission (SEC) to understand their position about the investor notes. By March 2008 it was clear that the SEC thought that the notes were in fact securities and so preparations were made to go through the registration process. So on April 7, 2008 Lending Club voluntarily shut down the investor side of their business.

This was a blow to Dan Ciporin and his team at Canaan Partners. They had looked at this issue closely and had come to a different conclusion. But by this stage it was clear that Lending Club had potential, their growth in the first quarter of 2008 had been outstanding. Despite this setback it was decided that Canaan Partners would steadfastly support Lending Club through the registration process. That was a good thing because the total cost in legal fees alone to Lending Club to go through the SEC registration process was $4 million.

During the SEC registration period no investors could sign up nor could existing investors fund new loans. However, Lending Club continued the borrower side of their business and funded borrower loans with their own money. Investors in existing loans would continue to receive payments into their account.

It was called a "Quiet Period" because during the process of SEC registration the management was forbidden from talking publicly about their company in any way. Lending Club even took it to an extreme when they won a Webby Award during their quiet period. They accepted the award with a banner that read: "Can't say anything. Quiet Period".

## The Financial Crisis

Lending Club reopened from their quiet period on October 14, 2008. Right in the thick of the worst financial crisis since the 1930's. By this time Lehman Brothers was in bankruptcy, Washington Mutual had just recorded the largest bank failure in American history, Wells Fargo had just bought the nearly bankrupt Wachovia and the list went on.

Needless to say this was not a good time to be trying to grow any kind of consumer finance business. People were scared. But Laplanche was undeterred. While there were days during the crisis where he was a little nervous, on the whole he saw the financial meltdown as an opportunity. In the news everyday it was being clearly demonstrated that the financial system was inefficient and dysfunctional. It was ripe for innovation.

With banks clearly not lending Laplanche saw a real opportunity for Lending Club – they could become part of the solution to the financial crisis. Everything that Lending Club had been doing for the past two years was now needed more than ever. It was with that frame of mind that Laplanche pressed on.

## Consolidating Their Position

In March 2008, the last full month before Lending Club shut down to investors to begin their quiet period, their loan volume was $4.15 million. They would not cross over that mark until August 2009, ten months after they reopened from the quiet period.

The reason for this slow comeback was primarily because investors were hesitant. There was a perception in 2009 that all of consumer lending was bad. Lending Club was battling against the perception that their borrowers could be lumped in with all the subprime borrowers that contributed to the mess in the first place. Also, there was not a long track record of returns even though the loans issued in 2007 had held up remarkably well during the financial crisis.

Laplanche and the team continued on with their plan. After burning through a large chunk of their Series A financing round for the SEC registration they needed another funding round in early 2009. Lending Club's Series B financing round was $12 million and closed in March 2009. It was led by venture capital form Morgenthaler Ventures with partner Rebecca Lynn joining Lending Club's board. Both Series A investors, Canaan Partners and Norwest Venture Partners also joined this round.

By the end of 2009 Lending Club was gaining some momentum. Every month that year had seen positive loan growth and Lending Club ended the year with over $7 million in new loans originated in December.

## The Birth of LC Advisors and the Attraction of Large Investors

In 2010 Lending Club started to see interest from a different class of investor. Some large investors were coming on board and they didn't want to do their own investing. These people and organizations liked the idea of investing in peer to peer lending but they wanted some kind of managed product.

So Laplanche and his legal team started doing some investigation into how they could structure this kind of offering. This meant going back to the SEC with another innovative idea and going through the registration process again, but this time for a separate entity. In November 2010 they registered LC Advisors as a registered investment advisor. Then in March 2011 they launched the Conservative Credit Fund (CCF) that invests in the lowest risk borrowers (A and B grade). Shortly thereafter they launched the Broad Based Fund (BBF) that invests across all loan grades.

LC Advisors gained momentum quickly. By October 2012 over $250 million had been invested in these funds.

## In 2012 the Floodgates Opened

Lending Club entered 2012 in a strong position. In 2011 they had moved to downtown San Francisco in the heart of the financial district, they had launched LC Advisors and made several key executive hires. But even Laplanche admitted that 2012 blew away even their high expectations.

In 2012 Lending Club received some excellent press with major articles in Forbes magazine, Bloomberg and the New York Times. Then there was John Mack. The former CEO of Morgan Stanley made a big splash when he announced that he was joining the board of Lending Club. Here was one of the leaders of Wall Street joining forces with the new guard of financial services. This certainly helped win over many people who were skeptical of p2p lending.

In February 2012 Lending Club crossed half a billion dollars of loans originated since their launch. It took them nearly five years to reach that milestone. Then, just nine months later, in early November 2012, Lending Club crossed $1 billion in total loans issued. It was also announced at this time that Lending Club was now cash flow positive so profitability was going to be just around the corner.

Another big development in 2012 was the closing of a $15 million equity investment from Kleiner Perkins, which also led to the appointment of Mary Meeker to the board of Lending Club. The really big news from this investment was that it valued Lending Club at a whopping $540 million. More large investors began to pay attention.

Lending Club made a change in late 2012 that pleased many of their large institutional investors. They temporarily set aside 20% of the loans on their platform (selected randomly) for large investors who wanted to invest in whole loans. This didn't please the retail investors at all but it was another indication of the growing demand for Lending Club notes from institutional investors.

# Chapter 3 – Lending Club Investors

The Lending Club platform allows investors the opportunity to invest in consumer loans and it is the largest such platform in the world. These loans are fixed interest investments that provide monthly payments to investors in the form of principal and interest.

Investors should note that these consumer loans made by Lending Club are unsecured, meaning there are no assets backing the loan. This is different to a home mortgage or car loan where a borrower default will result in an asset being sold and therefore some recovery for the lender. The leverage that Lending Club does have with borrowers is that they report all payment activity to the credit bureaus – so a late payment or a default will hurt the borrowers' credit score.

## Investor Eligibility

Not everyone is eligible to invest with Lending Club. The retail investment platform is only open to investors in certain states and there are also income requirements. Here is the official wording on eligibility from the Lending Club website:

*Individual investors can invest in Notes if they are a resident of: California, Colorado, Connecticut, Delaware, Georgia, Hawaii, Idaho, Illinois, Kentucky, Louisiana, Maine, Minnesota, Missouri, Mississippi, Montana, New Hampshire, Nevada, New York, Rhode Island, South Carolina, South Dakota, Utah, Virginia, Washington, Wisconsin, West Virginia, and Wyoming.*

*Investors who are residents of states other than California or Kentucky must have (a) an annual gross income of at least $70,000 and a net worth (exclusive of home, home furnishings and automobile) of at least $70,000; or (b) have a net worth of at least $250,000 (determined with the same exclusions).*

There are additional requirements for residents of California and Kentucky. Regardless of which state you reside in you are not allowed to invest more than 10% of your net worth in Lending Club.

These eligibility rules do change from time to time so you should check the Help section on the Lending Club website for the latest rules:
http://www.lendingclub.com/kb/

For investors that don't reside in one of the 28 approved states there is another option. Lending Club has a trading platform operated by FOLIOfn and residents in several other states are eligible to buy existing notes in this way. Below is a map showing the breakdown of investor eligibility. There is more information on the trading platform later in this chapter.

Lending Club Investor Availability by State

States Available for Investors
Foliofn Investors

# Lending Club Prospectus

The SEC regulates Lending Club so there is always a prospectus available for interested investors. You will find a link to the latest prospectus on the Lending Club home page. It is quite a comprehensive document, usually around 100 pages long, and it contains information about Lending Club and their investment opportunity.

There is a detailed description of the risks involved, common questions and answers, how Lending Club operates, some analysis of the loan history and much more. A thorough analysis of the prospectus will allow investors to make fully informed investing decisions.

In addition to the prospectus Lending Club also files quarterly reports (Form 10-Q) and annual reports (Form 10-K) with the SEC and these are also available for viewing on the Lending Club website.

## Types of Investor Accounts

There are several different account options available for investors.

### Standard Investment Accounts

This is a taxable investment account that any eligible investor can open with a minimum of just $25. The IRS will treat interest earned in a standard account as ordinary income.

### Retirement Accounts

For retirement accounts you can open a new IRA or you can rollover an existing IRA, 401(k) or other retirement account to Lending Club. To qualify for a no-fee IRA you must open the account with a minimum of $5,000, otherwise there is a $100 annual fee. To continue to qualify for the no-fee IRA after the first year, you must maintain a minimum balance of at least

$10,000. All retirement accounts opened through Lending Club's website are administered by a third party custodian, SDIRA Services, a subsidiary of Horizon Bank. With all retirement accounts there are no taxes due to the IRS on interest earned.

### Lending Club PRIME Accounts

If you like the idea of investing with Lending Club but you want a completely hands off approach then you can open a PRIME account. You decide the initial parameters on how you want to invest and then Lending Club does all the work for you. They will invest in loans on your behalf and can continue to reinvest all accumulated cash if you wish. The minimum to open a PRIME account is $25,000 and you can open a standard or retirement account as a PRIME account.

### Other Account Types

There are several other types of accounts available to investors. There are joint accounts, trust accounts, corporate accounts and accounts for minors (UTMA and UGMA). Investors should contact Lending Club about opening one of these alternative accounts.

## Investor Fees

Every time a borrower makes a payment Lending Club takes a 1% service fee that is deducted from each investor account. This fee is rounded up or down to the nearest cent with a minimum fee of $0.01. This fee is a fixed rate and will be charged on any payment whether it is a regular payment, partial payment or a loan payoff. This doesn't mean that your returns are reduced by 1%, in some cases it will be less.

Here is the explanation of how these fees work from the Lending Club site. This explains why the impact of the 1% fee is in fact less than 1% in most cases:

*We charge investors one percent (1%) of all loan payments. This service charge is designed to cover our costs for servicing loans, making Note payments and maintaining investor accounts. The 1% service charge impacts investors' annual returns by less than 1% because it is not an annual charge. The average impact of the 1% service charge on the annual returns of a 36-month Note is 0.72%, while the average impact on the annual returns of a 60-month Note is 0.41%. Here is the formula for calculating the impact of the service charge:*

*=RATE(36,monthly_payment\* 0.99,amount_invested)\*12-weighted_average_interest_rate for 36-month Notes and*

*=RATE(60,monthly_payment\* 0.99,amount_invested)\*12-weighted_average_interest_rate for 60-month Notes.*

*Example*

*Invest $100 at 10% over 36 months, you get a monthly payment of $3.23. The impact of the service charge is then calculated with "= RATE(36,-3.23\*0.99,100)\*12-0.1" This equals -0.6198%, meaning the investor would be getting a net of 0.62% less after fees due to the service charge. The investor's net interest rate would then be 9.38%.*

This assumes that a borrower makes on time payments for the duration of the loan term. If this happens then the impact will always be less than 1% on your returns.

You can see the fees impact on your account in one of two places – you can see the breakdown of every transaction on your Account Activity page and the monthly total when you look at your monthly statement.

# The Investment Platform

At Lending Club new loans are added on to the platform seven days a week. They are added in batches at 6am, 10am, 2pm and 6pm Pacific Time every day. Then as soon as a loan is 100% funded it is removed from the platform. This makes for a dynamic and ever changing marketplace for investors.

Investors basically have two choices when it comes to investing in loans. There is an automated portfolio builder, which allows investors to put their entire cash balance to work in just a few clicks. Then there is the manual method where investors invest in each loan individually. Both methods have a minimum investment requirement of $25 per loan.

## Automated Loan Picking With the Portfolio Builder

The Build a Portfolio tool is a popular way for investors to put money to work quickly. Even with a large amount of available cash investors can be fully invested in just four clicks.

It works this way. There is an Invest button on the Account Summary screen that provides investors with three options: a low, medium and high-risk option as shown below.

**Build a Portfolio** from 801 Notes

| Option 1 | Option 2 | Option 3 |
|----------|----------|----------|
| 10.86% | 14.89% | 19.9% |

Once you click on one of these options the tool will then build a portfolio based on your selections. Option 1, the low risk option will invest in mainly A and B grade loans. Option 2 will invest primarily in B and C grade loans with some A and some D grade loans as well. Option 3 invests in C, D, E and F grade loans.

If these three options are too restrictive there is a fourth option. The More Options button allows you to choose the exact target interest rate you would like and then it invests in the available loans that match your chosen rate.

## Selecting Loans Manually

When you click the Browse Notes link from the Lending Club Accounts screen you are presented with all available loans. There are typically somewhere between 500 and 2,000 loans available at any one time. When you click on a loan you are presented with a loan listing that will look something like this.

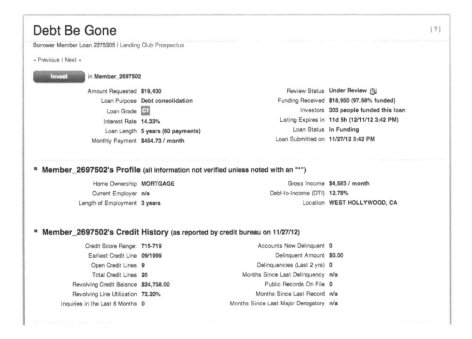

A loan listing contains five different types of information to enable investors to make an informed decision whether to invest or not.

1. The loan details – there is information about the loan itself such as the loan grade, loan purpose, interest rate, monthly payments, loan length and funding information.

2. Borrower details – while personally identifying details such as name, address and social security number are withheld from investors, information such as employer, profession, gross income and location are included.
3. Credit information – Lending Club pulls a complete credit report during the application process and shares much of this information, such as credit score range, delinquencies and credit line details, with investors.
4. Loan Description – filled out by the borrower to provide more information for investors. This field is optional and is sometimes left blank.
5. Questions and Answers – investors can ask predefined questions of the borrower and responses are available for all investors to see.

When investing manually investors can decide to lend any amount in multiples of $25. This can be done by just checking a box next to each loan and then clicking the Add to Order button. Then with just three more clicks the investor can complete the order.

## Loan Filtering

Reading the details of 1,000 available loans or more could easily become a full-time job. So, Lending Club provides loan filters where investors can choose to look at only those loans that are of interest. There are over 30 different criteria to choose from – typical filters are interest rates (presented as loan grades), loan terms (36 or 60 month loans), loan purpose, length of employment, loan size and credit score. By utilizing these filters investors can create a more manageable list of loans to consider.

Once an investor has created a set of filtering criteria these can then be saved for future use. Then every time the investor logs in to his or her account they can open this saved filter and run it on the current set of available loans. This can save a great deal of time and allows investors to put their money to work quickly.

Lending Club also provides a link to download all the available loans in a CSV file from the Browse Notes screen. Some investors prefer this method so they can run their own loan filtering in Excel. Every loan contains a unique URL that allows for easy investing with just a copy and paste from Excel.

## Net Annualized Return

Net Annualized Return

## 11.06%

The main account screen at Lending Club displays a Net Annualized Return (NAR) prominently. This number is the result of a somewhat complicated formula that reflects actual performance to date on the outstanding principal.

An important point to note about NAR is that it will vary. It reflects returns received on principal but when a borrower defaults that principal is deducted from your account balance – thereby reducing your NAR. Because of these defaults in most investor portfolios NAR reduces over time as the loans age.

Another thing investors should keep in mind is that NAR does not reflect your overall account performance, just the return of the money you have invested in notes. So, if you leave 50% of your account in cash your NAR may be 11% but the actual return on your total balance will be significantly less than that.

Because of this "cash drag" (it is impossible to stay 100% invested in notes all the time) most serious investors don't rely on NAR as the only measure of their investment performance. In reality it can often overstate actual performance, so to obtain a completely accurate measure investors can use the monthly statements provided by Lending Club. By doing some quick analysis in Excel using these numbers investors can learn their exact return on their Lending Club investment. There is more information about this here: http://www.lendacademy.com/xirr

## Portfolios and Account Details

When you make an investment in notes you have the option to assign the notes to a portfolio. Portfolios can be a very useful way of grouping your notes. For example, if you have two different strategies, one that is conservative and invests in only A and B grade loans and one that is aggressive and invests in only E and F grade loans you can separate these strategies into different portfolios.

Then under the Portfolios tab you can compare the different portfolios. Also, there are several third party tools that are discussed in the next section that will allow you to conduct in-depth analysis of your portfolios. This way you can see which strategies are providing the best returns over time.

Lending Club provides some analysis on your portfolios as well as your overall account. If you click on the More Details link on the main account screen you will be presented with something similar to the screen below.

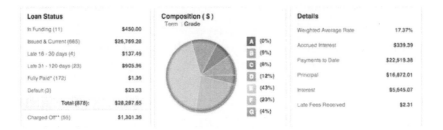

| Loan Status | | Composition ($) | | Details | |
|---|---|---|---|---|---|
| In Funding (11) | $450.00 | Term Grade | | Weighted Average Rate | 17.37% |
| Issued & Current (665) | $26,769.28 | | A (0%) | Accrued Interest | $339.39 |
| Late 16 - 30 days (4) | $137.49 | | B (9%) | Payments to Date | $22,519.38 |
| Late 31 - 120 days (23) | $905.96 | | C (6%) | Principal | $16,872.01 |
| Fully Paid* (172) | $1.39 | | D (12%) | Interest | $5,645.07 |
| Default (3) | $23.53 | | E (43%) | Late Fees Received | $2.31 |
| Total (878): | $28,297.65 | | F (23%) | | |
| Charged Off** (55) | $1,301.39 | | G (4%) | | |

There is a detailed breakdown by loan status of every loan in your account. You will also see a colorful pie chart that shows the distribution of your notes by loan grade or loan term. One of the most interesting numbers in the Account Details screen is the Weighted Average Rate. This tells you the average interest rate of all the notes in your account weighted by note amount. The difference between this number and your Net Annualized Return is due to the impact of defaults and service charges. Those details are also available on this screen.

## Third Party Investor Tools

While Lending Club provides some analysis of investor portfolios as well as their entire loan history it is considered inadequate by many serious investors. Luckily, an entire data analysis eco-system has been created around Lending Club that provides a great deal of information to investors. Since the entire loan history is available for public download some enterprising investors have created a way to query this data and back test various investment strategies.

1. **Nickel Steamroller**
   (http://www.nickelsteamroller.com/)
   Has a complete suite of useful tools for Lending Club investors. There is a Return Forecaster that provides a front end to the entire loan history of Lending Club broken down by loan grade. Investors can test various filtering strategies to determine the best historical returns. There is also a Portfolio Analyzer that allows investors to upload a file of their own notes from Lending Club and show projected returns broken down

by portfolio.

2. **Lendstats** (http://www.lendstats.com/)
   Was the first site to provide a complete performance breakdown of the Lending Club loan history. They also created a formula for projecting the real return of a portfolio by assigning loss rates to loans that are currently late but have not yet defaulted. When running filters it will also provide links to active listings on Lending Club.

3. **PeerCube** (http://www.peercube.com/lc/)
   PeerCube has two main functions. It provides an alternative to the Browse Notes section of Lending Club allowing investors to run more sophisticated filters. Then in just one click investors are taken to the Lending Club site to complete an investment on the loan. There is also a Peer Review section where PeerCube users can rate and comment on active loans that are in the funding process.

4. **Interest Radar** (http://www.interestradar.com/)
   Provides analysis of the loan history in a similar way to Lendstats and Nickel Steamroller. It provides a couple of unique tools for investors. There is a robust portfolio analysis section and there is also a "Strategy Shop" where the author shows some of the highest performing loan filters based on the historical data.

## Diversification

An investor who starts doing some research on Lending Club and p2p lending best practices will quickly come across the concept of diversification. The idea behind this is simple: investors who spread their money among many borrowers will likely experience lower volatility in their portfolio and reduced risk.

For example an investor with $20,000 to invest could put this entire investment into one loan or they could fully diversify this investment among 800 different loans (the minimum investment per loan is $25). Lending Club likes to point out that every investor with at least 800 notes has had positive returns. Below is a chart showing the breakdown of returns for investors with at least 800 notes.

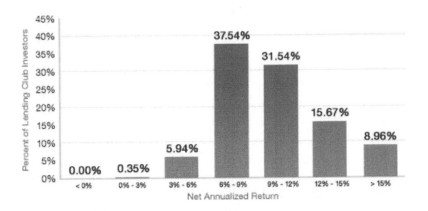

This chart shows that of the many investors (and there are thousands of them) who have 800 notes or more in their portfolio no one is earning a negative return and the vast majority of investors are earning 6% or more.

## Investment Returns

While Lending Club no longer provides an overall return number for their entire loan portfolio it does provide a return breakdown by loan grade. Below is a chart that was displayed on their website in November 2012.

This chart shows the average Net Annualized Return of each loan grade as well as the range of returns within each loan grade. These are not returns based on individual investor portfolios but rather on the loans themselves. So, if a portfolio of notes was created from the top 50% of the loans within each grade then the return would be roughly equivalent to the top dot in the chart. Conversely, if a portfolio of notes was created from the bottom 50% of the loans (this would presumably contain all the defaulting loans) then the return would match the bottom dot.

While this is quite a range of returns it is important to note that even picking just the bottom 50% of loans investor returns would still be positive. With a well-diversified portfolio of at least 800 notes it would be pretty much statistically impossible for an investor to only choose notes from the bottom 50%. But this chart does provide an idea of the range of returns likely within each loan grade for a well-diversified portfolio.

## The Trading Platform

When Lending Club launched in 2007 there was no trading platform. There was no way to sell notes; once you invested in a loan you had to hold that note to maturity.

But then came the SEC registration in 2008. The investor notes were now considered securities, in a similar way that common stock is considered a security, so they could now be traded on a secondary market.

Lending Club chose FOLIOfn to manage their trading platform. It brings a way for investors in most states to invest with p2p lending. Lending Club operates for retail investors in just 28 states but with the trading platform many more states are opened up. Only residents of the District of Columbia, Kansas, Maryland, Ohio, Oregon, and Vermont are ineligible for investing on the trading platform.

What the trading platform brought to Lending Club and p2p lending in general was liquidity. It provided a way for investors to liquidate their entire portfolio if needed. If an investor finds themselves in a bind and needing their money back as soon as possible they can sell their notes. As long as they are willing to sell their notes at a discount then they can likely liquidate an entire portfolio in just a few days.

With residents of many states only able to invest through the trading platform there is a ready market of buyers for these notes. Many investors have built very successful investment portfolios just by investing in the trading platform. At any one time there are tens of thousands of notes for sale ensuring a steady supply for trading platform investors.

## LC Advisors

LC Advisors, set up in 2010, provides a way for large investors to take advantage of Lending Club notes but in a vehicle that is more liquid and also contains bankruptcy protections. The two LC Advisor funds are held in a trust that is a bankruptcy remote entity that means if Lending Club were to go bankrupt then the investor money would be protected.

Initially the minimum investment in these funds was $100,000 and it was open to both accredited individual investors as well as institutional investors. These funds were private funds so there was no advertising of any kind to promote them; they relied on a sales team and word of mouth. In 2012 these funds had proven so popular, with tens of millions of dollars being invested every month, that the minimum investment was raised to $500,000.

While there is no public prospectus for LC Advisors there is plenty of publicly available information about them in Lending Club's SEC filings.

The Broad Based Consumer Credit Fund (BBF) invests across all loan grades in both 36-month and 60-month loans with an emphasis on grades B, C and D. This fund is like an index fund and mimics the overall breakdown of loans on the Lending Club platform. The Conservative Consumer Credit Fund (CCF) invests only in 36-month loans in grades A and B, with an emphasis on grade A.

LC Advisors is a wholly owned subsidiary of Lending Club and is registered with the SEC as an investment advisor. They charge a monthly management fee of between 0.55% and 0.75% (annualized) of the month-end balances. Neither fund participates on the trading platform.

## Collection Practices for Late Loans

The vast majority of borrowers pay on time every month. But sometimes a loan becomes late and when that happens investors need to rely on the collection efforts of Lending Club. Rest assured there is a vigorous collection effort conducted on behalf of the investors. What follows is an edited transcript of a conversation with the head of the collections team at Lending Club.

What is the process that is followed when a borrower misses a payment on their loan?

*"Because nearly all borrowers are doing ACH payments every month we know almost immediately if a payment fails. We then contact the borrower by phone and/or email to find out what is wrong – attempting to shape borrower behavior in the first contact attempt is critical. If that contact fails, we will generally continue trying for the next 30 to 60 days depending on a combination of the escalation behaviors such as no contact, refusal to pay, etc. If there has been no payment, we will outsource the loan to a third-party collections agency that can use even more advanced technology and tools. Note that, depending upon the borrower response (or lack thereof), we may hand off the loan even sooner than 30 days."*

Very occasionally a borrower will take out a loan and then never make a payment. This can cause a complete loss of principal for the investor. What does Lending Club do in these circumstances?

*"We take these situations, called 'straight rollers', very seriously at Lending Club. The first thing we look at is the viability of a collections lawsuit and post-judgment remedies such as real estate liens, bank levies, and wage garnishments if allowed in the borrower's state. If we believe we have a reasonable chance of recovery, we most likely will sue the borrower. We have dozens of judgments and stipulations to judgment out against borrowers at any one time and we will occasionally go to trial to secure payment."*

When a borrower declares bankruptcy is there anything Lending Club can do?

*"If a borrower has retained a bankruptcy attorney, we must immediately discontinue contact with them. We will typically charge-off the loan 60 days after notification of the filing. If we feel there is obvious fraud at work we may file a bankruptcy objection. (Note: this is very expensive and we need to be sure we have a solid case)."*

Investors sometimes wonder if the collection efforts vary between loans – such as more effort being put into the larger loans. Can you clarify this?
*Our collection procedure is uniform across all loans. The only time the size of the loan may matter is when we are deciding whether or not to take legal action – here a larger loan may make it more worthwhile to pursue in court.*

## Tax Liability on Lending Club Investments

Lending Club will issue a 1099-OID for any investor who earns more than $10 in interest plus late fees on any one note. Now, this is not $10 in total interest earned on the account it is $10 interest on any individual note. So, if an investor only holds $25 notes it is quite likely that they will not receive a 1099 from Lending Club because no note earned more than $10 in interest during the calendar year.

Just because you did not receive a 1099 from Lending Club, assuming you do have a taxable account, it doesn't mean your interest earned at Lending Club is tax-free. Even if you did receive a 1099 from Lending Club it is quite possible it will understate your total interest earned. The correct information as to how much interest and late fee income you received is included on Lending Club's year-end statement.

Investors who sold notes on the trading platform will receive a form 1099-B. This details all your transactions with dates, cost price, sale price and whether it is a long term or short-term gain.

It is always best when dealing with taxes to seek professional advice. Lending Club cannot provide tax advice so if you call them they will likely just point you to their online help about taxes.

## Investor Profiles

Investors in Lending Club come from all different kinds of backgrounds and they invest for different reasons. Here are some profiles of actual Lending Club investors who agreed to be interviewed for this book.

## Phillip McFarland

Phillip McFarland is a 28-year-old U.S. Army tank commander from Illinois who first read about p2p lending with Prosper in Money magazine back in 2006. He didn't open an account right away but he did some additional research and discovered Lending Club as well. But by the time he was ready to invest Lending Club was in their quiet period so he opened an account at Prosper. Then in 2009 after Lending Club emerged from their quiet period he decided to open an account there as well.

Initially Phillip didn't have any real strategy other than reading the loan descriptions and looking at the questions and answers. He would try and get a sense of the borrower by looking at their credit data, their income, and their employer. If there was no loan description then he would ask several questions and make sure they were answered to his satisfaction before investing.

As the number of loans on the platform grew Phillip realized he had to put some filtering in place. So he narrowed down the loans based on the following criteria: verified income, 3+ years of employment, no delinquencies and no public records. He also looks at amount of the monthly loan payment in relation to their gross income – he wants to make sure that the borrower will be able to easily afford the loan.

Phillip is a very active Lending Club investor. He logs on every day to look at the new loans that meet his criteria. He will always sort the available loans by time remaining so he only looks at the new loans that have just been added. He will spend 30-60 minutes every day on Lending Club.

He has a portfolio of around $25,000 invested in Lending Club and he typically invests $25 or $50 per loan, very occasionally putting in a little more.

Phillip has a second account that he uses mainly for investing on the trading platform. He has an interesting strategy here. He will look for late loans that are for sale on Foliofn that have a deep discount of 90% of more. He will invest in many of these loans with the hope that some of them will come back to current. He has only been doing this for a few months and he realizes this is a gamble so he only has a small amount of money in this account.

Like many investors he has most of his liquid investments in the stock market, some in a savings account and he even put some money into U-Haul Investors Club. But his Lending Club investment is the one that gets most of his attention and the investment that he enjoys the most.

His goal with his Lending Club account is to keep growing it to where he can make $2,000 a month in interest.

## Larry Ludwig

Larry Ludwig is a 41-year-old website designer and blogger (he runs InvestorJunkie.com) from New York and he has been a Lending Club investor since 2009. Larry's interest in Lending Club and p2p lending began as a result of the financial crisis. He saw fixed income annual interest rates go from 4-5% down to close to zero and decided to actively look for alternatives.

He discovered Lending Club after searching online for alternative investments. He was looking for an investment that would generate an income. He had known for some time that credit cards were a cash cow for banks so when he found a way to participate in consumer credit directly he became very interested. But he had some healthy skepticism so he started out slowly with a $1,000 investment.

Larry took a somewhat unique approach when deciding on a strategy for his Lending Club investment. He did some research on banks and what they considered to be a good profile for a credit card borrower. He also used the analysis tools on Lendstats.com and has read many of the articles on LendAcademy.com.

Larry doesn't use any of the automated tools that Lending Club provides. He manually selects loans based on his own analysis choosing filters based on the criteria that he thinks will reduce risk. He has two portfolios in his account – his first portfolio is medium risk focusing on grades B, C and D, but early in 2012 he decided to get a little more aggressive and now he invests primarily in D, E, F, and G grade loans.

He has pretty strict investing criteria:
- Only grades D, E, F and G
- 36-month loans
- Focused on debt consolidation loans
- Employment length of greater than one year
- Maximum debt-to-income ratio of 30%
- Credit score greater then 678
- No delinquencies in the past two years
- Verified income
- Reviewed by Lending Club

Even thought he has increased his Lending Club portfolio to well over $10,000 now it is only a small percentage of his overall portfolio. Most of his portfolio is in the stock market, he also has traditional bonds and bank CD's. As these CD's are maturing he plans on increasing his Lending Club portfolio over the next two years up to about 10% of his overall investment portfolio.

## Megan Nitz

Megan Nitz is a 32-year-old biodiesel engineer from Wisconsin who discovered Lending Club back in 2008 while reading a blog about alternative methods of borrowing money. It piqued her interest as an investment.

Megan is an engineer so she enjoys research. So for the next year or more she followed Lending Club closely. She watched while it shut down for SEC registration and when it opened back up she decided to open an account with just $100.

She started aggressively investing this $100 in four different G-grade loans after carefully analyzing various loans for several weeks. These four loans have now matured and she ended up with almost $140 in this account even with one loan that defaulted after about 18 months. Early this year she decided it was time to get more serious.

In February of 2012 she opened an IRA and deposited $10,000. She has invested the money slowly, taking nine months to be fully invested. She chose notes initially based on the recommendations of Ken from Lendstats.com who shared his loan picks on his forum. Then when Lendstats shut down she did some research on NickelSteamroller.com to test different investment criteria.

Megan wants to be fully diversified with 400 different notes before she will start to increase the note size from $25. But she doesn't want to have too many more notes than 400 because then she feels it becomes difficult to monitor everything.

She is an active participant on the secondary market. She will sell late notes at a deep discount depending on how late they are and she will also sell a note that has gone a little late and then comes back to current.

She will be putting next year's IRA towards Lending Club and would like to roll over the rest of her IRA money but she is hesitant to commit her entire retirement savings to Lending Club until they become profitable. Eventually, though, she would like to have enough in Lending Club to support herself and her husband.

Most of Megan's investments are in mutual funds that invest in the stock market. But she prefers spending time on her Lending Club investments. What she loves about p2p lending is that it makes something available to the small investor that has previously been only available to big hedge funds. It really democratizes the process of investing.

She hopes that her Lending Club returns will continue to perform well and that Lending Club will reach profitability soon. She also hopes that Lending Club will continue to cater to small investors and not give preferential treatment to institutional investors. If these things happen she will be moving more and more money into Lending Club.

# Chapter 4 – Lending Club Borrowers

The investor side of Lending Club is the one that gets most of the attention but it wouldn't exist without the borrowers. These are the men and women across America who have decided to forego the traditional forms of credit and take out a loan from their fellow Americans.

All Lending Club loans have a fixed term and a fixed interest rate so borrowers will know their monthly payment before they take out a loan. There are also no prepayment fees so borrowers may pay off their loan in full at any time with no penalties.

Borrowers may apply for any amount between $1,000 and $35,000. A second loan is allowed after six months of current payments but the total of both loans cannot exceed $50,000.

Like any loan application you have to disclose a great deal of personal information to Lending Club. This information is only used to make a credit decision and no investors are ever able to see any personally identifying information. Contact between borrowers and lenders isstrictly forbidden except through some preselected questions that investors may ask during the funding process.

## Eligibility

Not everyone is eligible to take out a loan at Lending Club. In fact close to 90% of applications are denied. There is quite a substantive list of requirements that all borrowers must meet before they will be considered for a loan.

1. Only residents of 42 states are eligible for a Lending Club loan. Currently Lending Club does not accept applications from Iowa, Idaho, Indiana, Maine, Mississippi, North Dakota, Nebraska, and Tennessee.
2. Must be a U.S. citizen or permanent resident of at least 18 years of age with a valid social security number.

3. Have a valid bank account.
4. A FICO score of 660 or above.
5. Have a debt-to-income ratio (excluding home mortgage) below 35%.
6. Have at least three years of credit history, showing no current delinquencies, recent bankruptcies (7 years), open tax liens, charge-offs or non-medical collections account in the past 12 months.
7. For credit scores of 740 and higher, you need to have less than 9 inquiries on your credit report in the last 6 months.
8. For credit scores below 740, you need to have less than 4 inquiries on your credit report in the last 6 months.
9. You cannot have maxed out all your credit cards – revolving credit card utilization needs to be less than 100%.
10. More than 3 accounts in your credit report, of which more than 2 are currently open.

Even if a borrower has met all of these requirements they may still be rejected for a loan because Lending Club mayask for and verify additional information from the borrower. In some cases they will demand more documentation,such as proof of income, from the borrower before making a decision whether to approve the loan.

## Loan Purposes

Borrowers must disclose their loan purpose during the application process at Lending Club. The most common reason to get a loan is to pay off high interest credit cards with a debt consolidation loan. Other purposes are loans for home improvements, small business, weddings, cars or for a major purchase.

# An Explanation of Lending Club Loan Grades and Interest Rates

Lending Club categorizes borrowers into seven different loan grades: A through G. Within each loan grade there are five sub-grades meaning there are 35 total loan grades for borrowers from A1 down to G5. Where a borrower is graded depends on many factors the most important of which is the data held in the borrower's credit report.

Lending Club will pull the latest credit report for every borrower and take the data held in that report and other factors such as loan amount and loan term to determine the interest rate. Lending Club is completely transparent when it comes to how they set these rates. There is a page on their site titled Interest Rates and How We Set Them (https://www.lendingclub.com/public/how-we-set-interest-rates.action) that discloses exactly how they determine the loan grade for every borrower.

Here is a quick summary of how Lending Club determines borrower interest rates. All this information is publicly available at the page mentioned above.

## 1. The Lending Club Base Rate
The base rate is the starting point in determining the interest rate for each loan. As of this writing the base interest rate at Lending Club is 5.05%. Now, no borrower can actually get that rate, this is just where their calculations begin. On top of that rate is added an adjustment for risk and volatility. There is a different adjustment rate for every loan grade from A1 to G5. This adjustment is added to the base rate to determine the final interest rate.

## 2. FICO Score
Initially every borrower is assigned a loan grade from A1 through C5 depending on their credit score. Borrowers with FICO scores of 780 and above are an A1 down to scores of 660-663 who are assigned a C5. But this is just an initial loan

grade – a borrower will likely be moved to a different grade based on the information described in the next two points.

### 3. Loan amount limits
Each loan grade has an upper "limit" for loan amount and if the borrower goes above that limit as determined by their loan grade (based on their FICO score) then they will be penalized. For example, a B2-grade borrower has a loan limit of $7,475. If this borrower wants a $15,000 loan they will drop four loan grades to a C1 and therefore pay a higher interest rate.

### 4. Other Risk Modifiers
There are other risk modifiers that will also send borrowers down a grade. Number of recent credit inquiries, the length of credit history, number of open accounts (ideal is 6-21 open accounts) and revolving credit utilization (ideal is 5-85%) are other items from a borrower's credit report that will impact the loan grade. Also, if the borrower chooses a 60-month loan term instead of 36-months this will send borrowers down a grade.

## Considerations Before Applying for a Lending Club Loan

When Lending Club launched back in 2007 the criteria for qualifying for a loan was not quite as strict as it is today. Back then if you had a credit score of over 640 you could apply for a loan. Today, you need a minimum credit score of 660 before Lending Club will even consider a borrower's loan application.

There are ways, as a potential borrower, that you can put yourself in a better position to qualify for a loan at Lending Club. Here are six points to consider before applying for a loan.

### 1. You must live in a state that allows borrowing
This one is a no-brainer but if you live in one of the following eight states you will not be allowed to borrow money from

Lending Club: Iowa, Idaho, Indiana, Maine, Mississippi, North Dakota, Nebraska, and Tennessee.

## 2. A High FICO Score is Important
On Lending Club the minimum credit score you need is 660. Your credit score goes a long way towards determining the interest rate you will pay with the very best rates reserved for borrowers with a FICO score of 780 or more.

## 3. Don't Shop Around for Credit
The number of times you have applied for credit recently (within the last six months) can have a dramatic impact on your interest rate and whether you are approved for a loan at all. For example at Lending Club if you have a FICO score below 740 and have more than three credit inquiries in the last six months then your loan application will be rejected outright.

## 4. Don't Apply for More Than You Need
If you need $10,000 don't apply for $20,000 because having the extra money would be nice. Only apply for what you need. As discussed in the previous section there are limits in place for every loan grade and if you go above these limits you will be penalized with a higher interest rate.

## 5. You Will Get a Lower Rate on a Shorter Term Loan
Loans from $1,000 to $15,975 are typically only available with a three-year term. But for loans of $16,000 or more you will have the choice of a three or five-year loan. For a three-year loan your interest rate will be lower, around 2.5% - 5% lower in most cases. If we take a hypothetical C-grade borrower with a $16,000 loan the rate would go from 17.77% for a three-year loan to 20.49% for the same amount in a five-year loan. It's a trade off between a lower monthly payment on a five-year loan but a higher overall cost due to the higher interest rate.

## 6. Don't Borrow in Round Numbers
Lending Club uses "Guidance Limits" when determining your interest rates. These limits vary depending on credit score but you can find yourself paying much more than necessary by

requesting a round number to borrow. For example, we will use our hypothetical C-grade borrower again. The Guidance Limit on C-grade borrowers is $12,500. But let's say this borrower wants to borrow $25,000. The amount of $25,000 is exactly 200% of their Guidance Limit and that will send the credit grade of the borrower down 10 notches. This might mean an interest rate increase from 15.80% to 21.49%. However, if they reduced the amount of the loan just $25 down to $24,975 the interest rate would be 20.49% or 1% less than the $25,000 amount.

This may sound confusing but it is all explained in detail on Lending Club's site here: https://www.lendingclub.com/public/how-we-set-interest-rates.action

Every borrower should spend 20 minutes studying that page before they take out a loan. It could save them hundreds or even thousands of dollars over the course of their loan.

## Borrower Loan Fees

There are no application fees, applying for a loan is free at Lending Club. But every borrower who successfully obtains a loan will pay a one-time origination fee.

### Origination Fee

This origination fee will vary depending on the loan term and the grade assigned to the loan. Below is a table that shows the different loan origination fees.

| Loan Term | A | | | B | C | D | E | F | G |
|---|---|---|---|---|---|---|---|---|---|
| Sub-Grade | 1 | 2 - 3 | 4 - 5 | 1 - 5 | 1 - 5 | 1 - 5 | 1 - 5 | 1 - 5 | 1 - 5 |
| 36-Month | 1.11% | 2.00% | 3.00% | 4.00% | 5.00% | 5.00% | 5.00% | 5.00% | 4.00% |
| 60-Month | 3.00% | 3.00% | 3.00% | 5.00% | 5.00% | 5.00% | 5.00% | 5.00% | 5.00% |

The origination fee is subtracted from the loan proceeds prior to disbursement. For example, if a borrower receives a $10,000 36-month loan and is assigned a loan grade of C1 then there is a 5% origination fee. Assuming the loan is 100% funded the borrower will receive $9,500 and Lending Club receives $500 of the $10,000 funded by investors.

## Late Payment Fee

Every borrower gets a 15-day grace period to pay their monthly loan installment but after that date a late payment fee is charged. This fee is the greater of 5% of the unpaid installment amount or $15. This fee is only charged once per late payment.

## Unsuccessful Payment Fee

When an automatic payment fails because the borrower's bank rejects the withdrawal an unsuccessful payment fee of $15 is charged to the borrower. Lending Club may make multiple attempts to process the loan payment and there is a $15 fee for each failed attempt.

## Check Processing Fee

Lending Club wanted all their borrowers to make automatic payments from their bank account – known as ACH payments. If a borrower decides to make a payment via check there is a $15 check processing fee per payment.

To avoid fees it is best for each borrower to maintain enough money in their bank account to cover the monthly loan withdrawal. For borrowers who may encounter financial difficulties it is always better to be proactive and contact Lending Club before the date of the loan payment.

One point that all borrowers should keep in mind is that Lending Club reports all of the borrower activity to the major credit bureaus so any delinquency or default will negatively impact a borrower's credit score.

# How the Borrowing Process Works at Lending Club

Applying for a loan on Lending Club is relatively simple and quick. If you know all your personal information the entire process should take about 10 minutes. Below is a step-by-step description of the borrowing process.

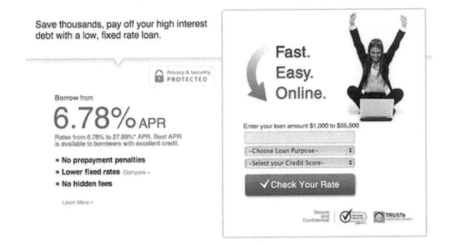

1.  **Enter the basics**
    To get the process started you need to enter three key pieces of information: the loan amount, loan purpose and your credit score. If you don't know your credit score you can just give an estimate. Lending Club will be pulling your credit report and won't just be relying on what you enter here. The reason they ask borrowers this question is that if a borrower knows their credit score is below 660 they will be advised that they should not apply for a loan. Lending Club will then provide some resources to help boost the borrower's credit score but they will not be allowed to continue with the loan application.

2.  **Enter Personal Details**
    The next screen is where you enter all your personal information such as name, address, date of birth, email

address and income. You also have to agree to the terms and conditions of the loan and the fact that Lending Club is going to pull your credit report in order to make a decision on your loan application. This is the same kind of information that is required on any credit card application.

3. **The Loan Interest Rate**
Now, the interest rate for the loan application is revealed for successful applicants. Here the screen displays the interest rate and monthly payment along with other loan amount options for the borrower. A borrower with good credit may be given an option to increase the loan amount. Also, if the loan amount is greater than $15,975 you will likely be given a choice of a three-year or a five-year loan term. All that is needed is for you to confirm the loan amount and loan term. For unsuccessful applicants a rejection notice is given here and an email is sent detailing the reason for the rejection. If the interest rate is not acceptable to the borrower they are under no obligation to accept the loan offer.

4. **Loan Details**
You need to create a loan title, preferably one that is descriptive so potential investors can decide at a glance whether to investigate this loan further. This screen is where employment information is entered as well as the borrower's social security number.

5. **Loan Rate and Terms**
This screen provides a Truth in Lending Disclosure Statement for the loan. This is the same kind of statement that is provided for home loans and car loans. Basically, it details everything about the loan: the annual percentage rate of the loan, the total finance charges, the loan amount, the origination fee and length of the loan. Much of this information will be dependent on the loan fully funding but any loan on the platform

that receives at least 60% of the funding amount will be made available to the borrower. Obviously, if the loan amount is not the same as the amount requested some of the amounts on the Truth in Lending Disclosure Statement will change.

6. **Link Your Bank Account**
   You must link a bank account to your Lending Club loan so that the loan payments can be deducted automatically every month. When you authorize Lending Club to verify your bank account they will actually do a small test debit on your account within a couple of days of applying for the loan. You need to then verify the exact amount that was debited and then your bank account is linked. Lending Club will then automatically deduct your loan payment every month.

7. **Loan is Listed on the Lending Club Platform**
   If you have followed the steps above your loan will be listed on the Lending Club platform within a few hours. Now, it is all about attracting investors so your loan can be fully funded.

8. **Create a Loan Description**
   Many investors read through every loan description so it is important to create a detailed description for your loan. The more information you can share here, particularly pertinent financial information, the better your chances of having your loan fully funded. If there is an anomaly on your credit report it is best to address it here rather than hope investors will ignore it.

9. **Answer Investor Questions**
   Investors can ask questions of the borrower during the funding process. These are not open-ended questions – but one of several preprogrammed questions pertinent to the category of your loan. A detailed and quick response to these questions will also increase your

chances of getting your loan fully funded.

### 10.     Loan Verification
Lending Club needs to verify several different pieces of information before your loan can be completed. Even if your loan is fully funded by investors, if you don't verify the information that is required by Lending Club, you will not receive your money and your loan will be deleted from the platform. Typically Lending Club will require you to verify your email and bank account as described in step 6. They may verify employment as well as income and a loan officer will likely place a call and have you verify various different pieces from your credit report.

This may seem like a somewhat complex process but it should only take 10 minutes to complete all these steps, maybe a little more if you don't have all the information at your fingertips. And the beauty of this kind of loan application you never have to leave your house. You just need a computer and Internet access.

## The Loan Funding Process

Once a borrower has posted a loan on Lending Club it will become available to investors. Loans can take from just a few hours to up to 14 days to fund with the average being 5-6 days. There are some very large investors now at Lending Club and it is possible for a loan to be funded by a small number of investors, possibly even just one investor. Depending on the loan amount, with larger loans having more investors, most loans are funded by 50-100 investors.

The good news for approved borrowers is that the vast majority of loans on Lending Club get fully funded. But if a loan is not 100% funded when the listing ends it will issue unless you inform Lending Club you want to withdraw your request.

Now, if your loan is less than 60% funded you have two choices:

1. You can accept the partial funding amount that you have received as long as it exceeds $1,000 and you do not live in Massachusetts. The options are more complicated for Massachusetts residents so those borrowers should contact Lending Club if their loan is not fully funded.

2. You may relist the entire loan request for another 2 weeks or relist the difference (subject to the limitations on size and interest rates). The loan amount and interest rate cannot be changed, but the loan title and description can be modified.

For loans that are less than 100% funded a new Truth in Lending must be approved containing your new loan terms. You will have four days to approve the new loan amount before money is returned to investors.

Just because a loan has been fully funded doesn't mean the borrower will definitely receive their money. Aloan can be fully funded by investors before the verification process has completed. If Lending Club finds a problem they can cancel the loan and the investors money is refunded.

Assuming verification has been completed to Lending Club's satisfaction and it is fully funded, the loan amount, less the origination fee, will appear in the borrower's bank account within 1-2 business days.

# Borrower Profiles

There have been nearly 100,000 borrowers who have taken out loans on Lending Club since they began in 2007. Here are profiles of three of these borrowers.

## Alex Taguchi

Alex Taguchi decided he was sick of being in debt. He had total credit card debt of $11,000 and wanted to pay it off once and for all. He liked the idea of having a fixed monthly payment knowing that at the end of the loan term his debt would be paid off.

He checked with his bank, Wells Fargo, and he was surprised to find that they would offer him a debt consolidation loan but at a 16.5% interest rate. He tried Bank of America as well but they rejected him outright. He decided to do some searching online for personal loans and he discovered Lending Club. He had never heard of p2p lending so he did some research and he liked the idea of borrowing money from a group of people rather than a bank.

He applied for a 3-year loan and was delighted when the interest rate quoted was 13.88%, well below what Wells Fargo had quoted him and below the rate on his credit cards. The application process was pretty straightforward, he provided Lending Club with the required information and watched as his loan was posted on the platform. Then it was a case of waiting.

After a few days his loan wasn't getting funded and he received a question from an investor to provide more information. He hadn't filled out a loan description or any details about his monthly expenses. Once he did that his loan was funded within 24 hours. This was back in late 2009.

He diligently made his $380 monthly payment for two and a half years before paying off his loan in full in early 2012 a few months ahead of schedule. He appreciated the discipline that comes from a fixed payment schedule and he is happy to report he is now free of credit card debt.

His experience with Lending Club was really positive. Since paying off his loan he hasdecided to become a lender and he now invests in other borrowers in a similar situation to himself.

## Dan Bradford

When he was a kid Dan Bradford's dad worked for Toyota. He was always bringing new cars home to test-driveespecially Land Cruisers. So, now as a hobby (and a profitable one at that) he restores old Toyota Land Cruisers. He often looks for them on E-Bay – ones that he can restore and then sell for a tidy profit. In late 2011 he found a 1977 Land Cruiser that had a lot of potential. When it came time to buy the car on E-Bay there was a financing option available that took him to Lending Club.

He went through the application process and borrowed $10,000 on Lending Club at 11.7% for 3 years. He explained in his loan description that he was putting up $12,000 of his own money for the car and just needed the loan until he could complete the restoration project and sell the car.

He finished his application process late in the evening. He woke up the next morning to find that his loan had been fully funded in six hours. He had the money in his bank account in less than a week. He sold the car six months later and paid off the loan in full.

So, for his next restoration project he went to Lending Club first. He found a rare 1981 diesel Land Cruiser from Japan so he took out a $20,000 loan. He decided on a 5-year loan this time, the lower payments give him more flexibility, even with a slightly higher interest rate. He still expects to have the loan completely paid off within 12 months. This particular loan was fully funded within two days with one investor taking 60% of the loan right off the bat.

Dan said that he didn't even consider other loan options. If he borrowed money on his credit card he knows his rate would be around 22% so that was just not an option to him. With Lending Club he gets a better rate and he has his money quickly.

Despite his positive experience Dan thinks this might be his last Lending Club loan. His financial situation is improving after some setbacks several years ago and he is looking forward to one day becoming an investor.

## Zachary Knight

Zachary Knight really wanted to finish flight training for his private helicopter license. But he didn't have enough money to pay for his lessons. He had used E-Loan in the past so he went back there and they quoted an interest rate of around 20%. He received an offer in the mail from Chase but when he filled out the application he discovered they wanted a rate of 33%.

So he started doing some research online and discovered Lending Club. He was a little wary because he hadn't heard of them before but he liked the concept. He applied for a 3-year $10,000 loan and was given an interest rate of 13%. While he liked the interest rate he was still unsure about it so he read the loan contract in detail and gave Lending Club a call to allay his concerns.

In the end he felt like the application was straightforward and transparent. He liked the simple loan contract that he could read and understand. His loan was funded within 14 days and he was able to use the money to finish flight school and get his helicopter license.

That was nearly three years ago. He has just a couple of payments left on his loan and if the situation arises he would definitely get another loan with Lending Club. He doesn't like giving his business to the big banks; he no longer has money with them. He liked the idea of paying interest back to his peers – people not that much different to himself.

# Chapter 5 – The Future

The future is indeed very bright for Lending Club and for peer to peer lending in general. There is almost a perfect storm of factors working in Lending Club's favor. Interest rates on fixed interest investments remain very lowcausing many investors to look at alternatives. Trust in the stock market is still low despite the recent gains for investors. At the same time credit card interest rates remain high. And of course, dislike of banks and Wall Street remains high.

## The Near Term Challenges

Lending Club is clearly taking advantage of the opportunities provided by the current financial climate. While these opportunities are large there are also some immediate challenges that need to be overcome before Lending Club can realize its potential.

### Becoming a Mainstream Investment

P2P lending is still a long way from becoming a mainstream investment. If you ask the average investor if they have heard of Fidelity or Vanguard most will answer yes. Ask these same people if they have heard of Lending Club or even the concept of p2p lending and you will likely get a blank stare.

There are occasional articles in mainstream media such as the New York Times, Forbes and The Wall Street Journal but there is not enough coverage yet to bring it to the awareness of the masses.

The appointment of John Mack, former CEO of Morgan Stanley, to the board of Lending Club certainly gained the attention of Wall Street. That news was covered by all the major financial publications, which meant the investment banking community had now heard of Lending Club.

Financial advisors, for the most part, are still unaware of Lending Club so very few are recommending this new asset class to their clients. Lending Club has been working with Fidelity and Charles Schwab to allow the clients of those companies to invest through LC Advisors. But the options for smaller investors are limited.

The average investor cannot go along to Vanguard or Fidelity and invest in a mutual fund that invests in Lending Club notes. If and when that happens it is safe to say that Lending Club will have become a mainstream investment.

## The States Problem

If you have $500,000 to invest you can be a resident of any state and invest with Lending Club through LC Advisors. But if by chance you don't have that much money to invest and you want to invest directly through the Lending Club retail platform you must reside in one of the 28 approved states. Until they can allow investors on the retail platform from large states like Texas, Pennsylvania and New Jersey they will have difficulty gaining nationwide appeal. Sure there is the secondary market for some of these states but many investors find it cumbersome and unwieldy. Unless the interface is completely overhauled there it will only ever have limited appeal.

The problem is that every state has their own separate securities laws and Lending Club has to register with each state one by one. What Lending Club needs is some kind of federal law that overrides these state laws. This kind of law may be forthcoming in the future – the JOBS Act that was passed in early 2012 could be a catalyst for change in this area. But this is likely several years away.

## Institutional Versus Retail Investors

When it comes to the investing side of the business Lending Club must satisfy two groups of investors who sometimes have competing goals. Institutional investors want to fund large portions of loans or even entire loans. They are investing large amounts of money and they expect to be able to put their money to work quickly.

Retail investors were the driving force in the first few years of Lending Club. They invest small amounts of money but they consider themselves the true heart of p2p lending. They dislike any special treatment shown to institutional investors and are worried that eventually they will be squeezed out as more big money is attracted to Lending Club.

In late 2012 Lending Club has indicated that about 50% of their investor money comes from retail investors and 50% is from large institutions. Clearly, it is in their best interests to keep both groups happy. If this ratio is to remain steady going forward, and the management at Lending Club have indicated that is their goal, it will require a delicate balancing act.

## Getting to Profitability

Lending Club is on the verge of profitability but they have never had a profitable quarter (as of late 2012). Like many disruptive companies that are creating new industries (like Amazon.com in the 1990's) it has taken a long time to build up enough momentum to be profitable. While Lending Club is very well funded and has plenty of cash on their balance sheet, many investors want to see a profitable business model before they are willing to commit large amounts of money.

The good news is that Lending Club announced in November 2012 that during the third quarter of 2012 they were cash flow positive. So profitability should be just around the corner. This is a good thing for Lending Club and the industry as a whole.

When they do reach full profitability there will likely be a flood of new investor money.

## Long Term Opportunities

The opportunities for Lending Club are many. The biggest one is continuing to focus on unsecured consumer loans. According to the Federal Reserve (http://www.federalreserve.gov/releases/g19/Current/) the total revolving consumer credit market was worth $855 billion in August 2012. Lending Club has less than 0.1% of this market so there is clearly a lot of room for growth.

### Future Product Lines

While Renaud Laplanche has indicated that he will continue to focus on unsecured consumer loans for quite some time he has also said that he would like Lending Club to expand into other loan products eventually. He thinks Lending Club can be a partner to consumers through various stages of their life.

This means expanding into such products as student loans, auto loans, home mortgages, home equity lines of credit as well as small business financing. Laplanche has said there is no limit to what the platform can handle in terms of consumer credit.

He is really talking about a paradigm shift away from banking. Laplanche believes that banks have served a useful purpose to centralize capital, to aggregate a large amount of capital, and redistribute it. Now, technology and the Internet make that function unnecessary. And Lending Club can make capital flow more efficiently and more directly between the source of capital and the use of capital. That is their central premise and one of the reasons why they are becoming so successful.

# The Lending Club IPO

Laplanche has stated many times that there are no specific plans for an Initial Public Offering (IPO) of their stock – they are happy to be an independent company. But Lending Club may do an IPO sooner rather than later for an interesting reason.

When Lending Club becomes a public company and their securities are traded on the stock exchange they qualify for what is called a "Blue Sky Exemption". This means that the state securities laws no longer apply and retail investors will be eligible to invest in Lending Club from any state.

Unlike most companies that use an IPO primarily to raise capital a Lending Club IPO could have a different goal. While the money generated from an IPO will certainly be useful, particularly for the venture capital partners who have put in many millions of dollars over the years, being available toinvestors in all 50 states would be a tremendous boon to Lending Club.

So an IPO for Lending Club would be more important from a marketing standpoint than for just raising money. IPO's from fast growth companies often get a lot of attention from the mainstream media and Lending Club would likely be no exception.

Investors from many of these ineligible states, many of whom will have been waiting for several years to become an investor, will come flocking to the platform. The months following an IPO would likely see huge increases in investment inflows to Lending Club.

But as Laplanche has said many times an IPO is not on the near term horizon. Still, it will likely happen one day and when that day comes Lending Club will become a mainstream investment.

## A Trillion Dollar Company

Lending Club has maintained at least a 100% growth rate since their founding in 2007. This rate of growth has accelerated in 2012. But if, and it is a big if obviously, Lending Club can maintain a growth rate of 100% through the end of the decade they will have originated around $200 billion in loans by January 2020.

So taking a long-term view, even if the growth rate does slow down, within 20 years it is quite possible that Lending Club will have issued over a trillion dollars in loans. If that happens this remarkable company will have truly changed the face of consumer finance forever.

## About The Author

Peter Renton is an entrepreneur who has started and sold several companies in the printing industry. He is now a full time blogger and publisher of the most widely read blog about the p2p lending industry called Lend Academy (http://www.lendacademy.com/). He is also the creator of the popular video course, the P2P Lending Wealth System (http://www.p2plendingwealthsystem.com/), that teaches investors how to maximize their returns at Lending Club and Prosper.

While he has no formal qualifications he is a lifelong avid investor and firm believer in p2p lending. He writes several times a week about p2p lending including extensive coverage of the two leading companies Lending Club and Prosper. He also regularly shares his investment returns and the balances of each account for the world to see:
http://www.lendacademy.com/returns

You can connect with Peter Renton and Lend Academy in many places:
Twitter: https://twitter.com/LendAcademy
Facebook: https://www.facebook.com/LendAcademy
YouTube: http://www.youtube.com/lendacademy
LinkedIn: http://www.linkedin.com/in/peterrenton

Printed in Great Britain
by Amazon.co.uk, Ltd.,
Marston Gate.